1

SONGS FOR MY FATHER

100 POEMS OF HOPE TO GOD

LOLA AHMED

PUBLISHING
CHRONICLES

To my God and Father! May these songs be a sweet sound to your ears. May your presence touch each soul as we sing each moment. Thank you for your presence.
And to you... may this poetry collection be another source of courage to fight and stand in all seasons...

CONTENTS

INTRODUCTION

Beauty is not about perfection! It is also the ability to flourish amid thorns and roses, embracing the beauty in each season.

— LOLA AHMED

Through stabs and slabs......
Fiery furnaces he puts out,
peace and joy as we walk with him,
and he... with us!

Be well, embrace each journey, and embrace the courage to never give up in any season. These are songs for my father!

"Just breathe, for a minute…
for a second…
and many more
Just fight, one more time….
and speak life in all
Just live one more day. Yes, there are
many more to come!
Just dance…
to the rhythm…. the lions retreat!
Just sing…
for my father… his heart is love
Just breathe, one more time, in hope and
love."

— FEBRUARY 2, 2024

ACKNOWLEDGEMENTS

I wake up each day
Speechless to the love
You've given me.
I look back and see
How you have covered me
Not because of who you are.
You are my father.
Silent screams and shouts
To show you how grateful I am for each passing moment
Like an oracle, my voice speaks your words from the core of
my being....
Your love and your grace in my story
Your glory, inexplicable
You are a good father
The greatest of all, the father of fathers
You are God and God alone
No one knows me like you do...
No one loves me like you do
I dedicate this book of songs from my heart to you
So others may derive inspiration from how you

Held me! Never let me go and brought me
Out from a bottomless, dark pit and back into your presence.
These songs are from my heart to you.
These are Songs for my father!
I invite you to sing a song with me...
to the father...

— July 14, 2017

PROLOGUE

Sinking in and out of dark hollows
No rainbows in sight
No birds chirping
I looked up to you
I cried out to my father
Day and night, night and day!
Could I tell the difference?
In pain and out
How did I make it through? You ask!
His presence soothes my soul
Though my heart may seem frail
His strength, his love, and his peace are divine
with songs in my heart each day
I sing 100 songs to you.

Some in pain, most in joy and hope
You heard my cry; you hear each heart!
Do not ask me how... I am but an awesome mortal
The most awesome of all is my father.
I call him father!

PART ONE

THUNDERSTORMS

1-10

WAKE ME UP

— MARCH 26, 2017

Wake me up to your presence.
I need you once again.
Wake me up
The plague of curtains knocks once again.
Wake me up!
I need to live again.
My heart is in a stormy wave.
Body and soul Weak...
I need your strength to live.

IN BATTLEFIELDS

Wake me up to your presence.
Wake me up to your praise.
Wake me up
So I may live.
The plague of dissolution
Gnaws at my heart
My mind, my soul
In battlefields
Of blood and sand
Of wars untold...
What will unfold?
In battlefields

LOLA AHMED

My sight on you
Please wake me up
Do wake me up
To sing your praise
In battlefields.

FREE MY SOUL

My heart is heavy, body and soul
Weak and frail.
I need your touch
My heavy heart
My heavy soul
Through veils, I push.
To live again
I look to you
My savior's breath
I breathe for you
Please walk with me
And free my soul.

SONG TODAY

~

I woke up with no song today.
My heart is frail deep in my soul
I'm immersing in this abyss
I'm drowning; would you lift me again?

~

I woke up with no song today.
Your love for me, I still do feel
In deepest pain, I see your face
Your voice is faint
Please walk with me.

I woke up with no song today
dependencies and patterns held me bound
Bound to my bed, down to my knees
I'm sinking deep; please lift me up
I woke up with no song today.
conflicts held me bound; you cleansed my soul.

NEVER CEASE

My love for you will never cease
Through pain and cravings.
I will still praise
I will pray, I will speak.
I will share... Your word is love.

In dormant times, fear was brought in
Fear was brought in, and pain followed suit
In the pits, I found myself again
My mind, my heart, my soul!

Your dwelling place
My love for you, I can't compare
Your love for me...
I hold too dear.

MY HEART BEATS AGAIN

~

My heart beats
It's a brand new day
I am aware!
The rhythm of my heartbeat
The rhythm of life...
Light all around me
Hollowness... darkness
I see... No more.
The love of Christ
I cannot describe
His love for me
I did not contend
Neither brawl nor strive

Did I... to earn his love
Lots are cast for my sake
Yet he holds me close
I walk towards the cliff
He brings me near
Back to him
Back to me
He holds me close.
I'm away from the cliff
His light is back in me
His light still shines on me
Like a butterfly...
My heart beats again.
It is a brand new day!

DAYS OF GRACE

~

Today is another great day!
To give thanks to my father.
The guerilla showed me a grave.
The Lord showed me his face.
Darkness and veils
He is taking away
Love and honor
He clothed my face
My faith in my father
My passion blossoms each day.
Like time's past
But this time, more
Shame and pain

Drove me from your side
In my pain, I ran away.
Now I run back
With all that's in me.
All I need is your grace, your presence
All I need is you.

LET THIS CUP PASS OVER ME

~

In pain and anguish
I hope and pray
Let this cup pass over me.
This pain is just too much to bear
This pain I need so far away
Let this cup pass over me.
In my delusions
and fallacies... did I fall?
In pain, missteps, in anger bade the fall?
Do lift me; do take the pain away
Do take this giant, and let me live
Do breathe in me
Once more, all the more

Do bring me to life once again
In life, I'm yours
In pain, I'm yours
This temple is all yours.
In Slaying Giants...
Let this cup pass over me.
This I pray!

DWELLING IN YOUR PRESENCE

❧

In your presence is where I want to be
In your presence, I need to be
Your temple, your dwelling place
Don't leave this temple lord
Come and dwell fully once again
Come alive once again
Dwell in this temple once again, father
In your presence is peace!
In your dwelling place, strength!

The sight of weakness
Your strength in me
Without your presence...
What is, or is to be?
Who is man without you!
Who am I without you...
Come sweep over your dwelling place
Come soothe our souls once again!

BREATHE IN ME

Another brick road
Another roadblock
So many tug at my being
The cause to live
The will to live
Please breathe in me
The strength to stand
In pain and hurt
In sorrows cave
I take a step, another step.

Another brick road
Another roadblock
In you, I trust, not in my sight
...or might!
A mountain bricks
A thousand caves
A leap of faith
I'll walk with you...

MOUNT IN PAIN

Another day in pain
Another day, no gain
In sickness and strength
I will stand and fight.
This battle I fight so hard.
With no strength, so sad
In sickness and in health
I will hold on to grace.
The battles I've overcome
Left them all behind
My dreams right ahead...
Yet pain holds me back.
The veil unfolds; my dreams I see
They've pushed me thus far
My father's hand I hold.
Another day in pain
But mount I will.
Mount in pain, mount through pain.
In joy and praises, all day long.

PART TWO

I HEAR THE SOUND... OF GRACE

11-25

GIVING ME

What I have
I do not own
If I give
It's not my own...
The Lord provides
And he gives...
Who am I to hold back...
If I give!
He's given me
If I don't...
He'll make a way...
What I have is not my own
Where I stand

He's given me...
If he gives
Why do I lack?
All I know
He's paid the price.

MY SPIRIT LONGS: VISITATION

My spirit is frail
It fades with the wind
Dancing to the tune of the clouds
The cloud sways
In retrospect
Of nature's hymn!
To bring back life.
My spirit longs
The roses bloom...
For the king's home
His visits... to me in times past
My spirit longs...
He'll visit me.

And when he does
The wind will fade.
My heart will sail.
This preserved life
My spirit longs
He'll visit me.

GRACIOUS PEACE

Oh gracious peace
Please come to me
Do hold me close
And draw me near.
My father's hand
Doth shine on peace
His peace and love
Does hold me near
Oh gracious peace
Do dwell in me.

SAVIOR'S FEET

~

Strength and courage
In Christ, I find
Darkness knocks folly
and beacons my heart
Cliffs and ropes hang near me now
My Soul, he fights so hard to squash
Strength and courage I find in Christ
In weakness and pain
I see no soul
Blurry visions
Frail.... This heart
frail, but still, he fights to keep
My mind in pits so deep I screech

The Soul the Reaper fights so hard to squash
If frail, then why so hard he fights?
My keeper lurks, yes, in the pits...
My Soul, he keeps
My strength? His strength...
I look up and see my savior's feet.

DIGGING DEEP

In darkness and pain
Your grace abounds
In pain and grief
Your mercy speaks.
When all doors are shut
You open another
Or create one...
In all, I can phantom.
I can never fully describe
Your love and its depths
All I can and will say is....
God is good... All the time.

THE SOUND OF RAIN

~

I hear the sound of rain
All I see around is pain
In infirmity and strive
Through life's matchbox
I tried to break free
I've tried a million times
Fought a thousand times.
On angels wings
Now I lay.
I lost my life
To find you again
I am at your feet
At Jesus' feet

I lay each day
Till you pick me up again
And I'll see the rain.
I'll feel it through my fingertips
I'll live in it, in you...
I'll sing to you always.

MY STRENGTH IN YOU

~

Strength and courage
In you, I find...
Hope and Faith
Slips far away...
The strength to live
The grace to stand
The hope to fight
It's all in you...
You give me strength.
Your grace is here
You show me who I am each day
I lost my faith
My strength and zeal

This wilderness is far too dense
Lingering and callous... I am weary
I lost my strength
In the battlefield
The darts and stones do pierce my heart.
They pierce my soul
I'm out of breath...
I lay me down
With arms stretched out.
I stretch to you
I lean on you.
All strength is gone
But strength is you...
My strength in you
My hope is you...
Your everlasting open arms
You are my love
You are my life.
Though I am weak
You are my strength.
My strength in you, through battlefields.

THE PROCESS

I am not who you see.
I am not what you feel.
The process...
A journey we all take in life
I stand, I fall, and I stand again
I fly, I soar...
to crash and burn
The Fiery coals, the chimney slope.
Picked by your grace,
I see your face.
You lead me through this process map
The light does fade
But I see you...
In everything, in every way
Your grace, your voice, your mercy speaks.
And I recall...
This is not who I am
This process that threatens your light
This interruption in my walk with lilies
Lilies turned thorns
Thorns in roses
But In grace, I sing your song all day long.

HOLD MY HAND

Please hold my hand, for I am scared
The road seems just too far ahead
In sickness, still do hold my hand
For I will praise you all the same.
Please hold me close, for I am weak
Your strength I need now all the time
You breathe in me
And I see life
Please breathe in me so I'm alive.
Hold my hand. I need your touch
Your presence in my heart always
Though I am frail
Your strength in me
You love me all the same each day!

PRAISING YOU

I will praise your name.
Each day
As the sun rises
As I rise.
I will praise your name.
As the moon sets
I will praise you
In my weakness...
In sickness and strength
I will bless your name!
I will let the world know
That you are good
All the time
Oh lord! My strength
I will praise you
In the darkness, into the light.

YOUR PRICE, YOUR GIFT

~

Your price, your gift
Your love, I see
In many ways
In special ways
This humble heart
With tongue rolled tight
Your loving arms
You touch my heart
Your precious gift
The price you paid...
With open arms
I'll lift you up
Your love is sure
Your presence real...
My father gave this gift to me.

ALIVE AGAIN

Deep in my bones
Deep in my heart
Through pain and gain
I'll feel alive again.

Through the deep pits
Though chains hold me back
Through valleys and shadows
In dungeons bleak
I'll feel alive again.

In the deep of the pit
In the dead of the night
Out of the deep, he brought me.
Into the light of his arms
Into the love... his love.

Out of the pits, he brought me.
Into the light...
I am alive again.

REDEEMED

The spirits did come for me.
But send them back. I did
The silhouette by my bedside
A figment or.... Fact?

The spirit came for me.
Like the wind
I did see....
I did feel
I do know
I felt their presence here.

The spirit did come for me.
And send them back. I did

Their mistake, not mine, to take
Yes, flee away, I command this day.
Redeemed in Christ, resurrected with Christ.
My father's presence is here with me
The spirits flee, and my heart sings!

ARISE AND BUILD

Arise and build... he said!
My thought and strength is laid.
To rise in weakness
Is life's own meekness...
Arise in pain?
Arise in shame?
Where is the gain?
Life's only hope...
Like melting ice on Sunset Beach
The pain will surely fade away.
To stand is gain.
Through pain and shame
Arise and build
He said to me.

WHEN ALL IS GONE

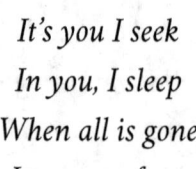

It's you I seek
In you, I sleep
When all is gone
I see your face.

It's you I seek
In you, I rise
When all is gone
You lift me up.

In you, I'm healed.
It's you, my strength.
When all looks bleak
It's you, I see.

In you... my hope
In you... my life
With all backs turned
I seek your face.

In you... My love
I find my peace
When all is gone
I see your grace.

PART THREE

THE SOUND OF FAITH

26-40

WHEN CAST DOWN

Stand still I will
When cast down.
My steps he leads
My breath, he heals
On surface low
He lifts me up.
Cast down, I am
Cast down I was!
My step he leads
My heart, he heals.
Cast down, I was
He makes me stand
He holds my hand and draws me near.

I CALLED UPON THE LORD!

I called upon the lord.
And he answered
In darkness and pain
Trials and shame.
I called upon him
He set his sight on me
Placed his hand on me
And I feel free
I want to be free
I need to be free.
I am free
So I called upon the lord
And he answered

But I wonder
How free I am
I ask! Because I feel the chains
My heart is frail
And I... in pain.
I called upon the lord.

STILLNESS

~

Strength as rain
Days as chaff
In stillness
Comes more rain.
Tears and rain?
When all seems lost
When strength is frail
In stillness
Grace shall reign.
With foresight veiled
With mountains stain
In stillness

Shall boldness prevail?
With routes unclear
And flight plans fear
In stillness
My father is here.

SPEAK NO GUILE

~

The voice in the wind
The depths of the sea
Mysteries unsolved
Secrets untold.
What will unfold!
The hope of today
With the faith of a morrow...
In all, we see
In all we do.
The fathers' touch
A courteous nod

LOLA AHMED

A gentle smile,
The love for life.
Do speak no guile!

PROMISE OF FAITH

~

In times past
In times present
In times to come
All things remain beautiful.
The beauty in pain
The virtue of hope
To live each day
Through the knowledge of Christ
His grace and peace
Compares to none...
Precious promises
We hold on in faith.

NOT BY SIGHT

~

In strength and love
The fight to be whole
With all that seems bleak
My hope is still you...
The sights of life
I look away...
But sighting fear!
In doubting gears...
I look away from fear.
He robs away my gain.

He steals away my flame.
And leaves in me the pain.
I stare right into his face.
My faith is back again.

MY GOD IS GOOD TO ME

~

Another day is here.
Another day to praise
To sing and shout in joy
My heart longs to rejoice.

~

Through grief and pain...
I live to praise him still.
In gladness, I will sing.
My God is always good.
He is good to me!

Through pain, he stood by me.
In pain, he stands with me.
In darkness and tears
My God is good to me.

In weakness, I will sing.
In darkness, I will praise
Aberration... I will say
My God is good to me.

Provider, yes he is...
Redeemer always is...
His light doth shine in me.
His love does shine on me...
My God is good to me.

WHEN I CALL

~

He answers when I call.
In days of grief
And scales of strive
He's here with open arms.
In pain through pain
With every dart
In him, I see
Peace at his feet.
Joy in his arms...
Each time I call
He gives me peace

Through weary storms
He gives me grace.
Each passing day.

GIFT

A gift I received
A privilege I perceived
This privilege I took
With arms wide open.
A gift, yes, it is
And savor it, I will.
This gift from you
Is precious...
More precious than
Rubies and gems.
Your grace carries me.
I will praise you always.

PURE HEART

My heart is pure
In pain, I see
Deceit and lies
Secrets are mine
You keep my heart
You hold my hands.
Chaos in mind
I'll live, I will.
Darkness around
Lots cast about
My heart is pure
Do keep my soul.

HEART OF PEACE

A heart of peace
A mind for peace
In all I seek.
Like dew upon the mountains
The precious ointment upon my head
A horn, a unicorn
The voices I hear
Beaconing to darkness
Clouding my heart
The darkness I see
So close, so close to me
The voices in my head
invoking darkness.
I choose the light
My heart for peace
My mind on peace.
His heart of peace
My heart entwines.

NEW DAWN

The new dawn is here
A new day is here
My father is near.
Open heavens beacon me
Limitations phantom me...
Healing rain falls down on me.
The pain I see no more...
The gain I see for sure
The dawn is here
My father near.
Your voice I seek each day
Your touch I long to feel.
Your voice to hear
Your heart to touch...
A new dawn is near
My father says to me...
Seek his face; I do
Arise and build, he says.

THIS MOUNTAIN

Looking at this mountain
In God, we trust
Its static build
Seductive lips.
Looking at this mountain
An everlasting stance
Unshakable pride
Remarkable strength
Looking at my mountains
God's open arms
His loving grace...
In God, I trust.

PIERCING VOICE

To pierce the soul of a king
To strike the sky with thunder
Words unspoken
Words spoken forth
Striking forth...
A voice in the wind
A voice in the wilderness
A wanderer through many storms
Oceans arise
Portions aside
Piercing of the heart
Shackles on the feet
Shackles broken, potions destroyed
This voice speaks once again
The voice of the traveler
The voice of peace.

THIS VOICE WILL SING

A song from my heart
A song from my soul
In the midst of this battle
This voice will sing
Though croaked and cracked
When darkness comes
This voice will sing
In faith, in hope.
The battle for this soul
This anointed one
Fallen in a pit
Where darkness prevails
This voice will sing
This soul will dance.
He hears my voice
And lifts me up.

PART FOUR

SEEKING PEACE FROM WITHIN

41 - 55

I'M ON MY KNEES

I once cried and sang with joy
A song I love so much
"Bring me to my knees."
hit me on the head
Bring me to my knees: la-gi-mo
I wish I hadn't sung...
Now, I am on my knees.
Deep inside a pit
Your love still keeps me safe...
Your praise is still on my lips
Your grace, your love, your strength
I see in all that's near and far...
Though this is hard to bear

I sing with joy through dread...
and even on my knees
Oh, Lord! It's hard to breathe
Rise up down here, I pray!
You light to shine on me
I'm on my knees right now
Lead me to your secret place
as I abide in you
I'm on my knees with faith.

OLD CROSS

~

I cling to your old, rugged cross
Through crowded, clouded mind
I have no strength to fight
Forgive my treacherous ways
Forgive my crafty thoughts
Please lead and teach, I ask.
In faltering, father lead
In altering, heal my soul
Do take me where you will
Been streaming far too long.
Though scary... what I see
I'll always be your child

Don't leave me in this pit
I feel your peace here... I praise
I place my hands in yours
I'm on my knees with joy.

RISING

~

Scourge of the earth
Scorned by the soil
Relinquished in the dark.
A soul cries out
Desolation of the mind
Agony, this frame is in
Terror in the day
Dread comes with the night.
The horror, the panic
The wish...
"It's just a mirage."
The torment, a figment
The miseries... an illusion...

or just a figment.
The vision of resilience
Rising from the ashes
Through the agony
I see you.

YOU CARRY ME

~

My desires drift as pods.
My expectations seep away.
The thief in the night
Knocked on my door
And I opened...

~

Walking towards his beautiful torso.
He stretched out his arm.
His hands invited me in
I saw you silently watch me.

But as in a trance...
I stretched out my hand and held his.

The thief in the night stole
my heart in chaos,
my mind was in disarray
My body pierced beyond mending?
In agony, I look to you!
You smiled and stretched your hand.
I held it... I'm restored
You carry me.

STRONG RIGHT ARM

~

In despair, I was
With nowhere to run
Roadblocks ahead
I held on to the wheels
In my strength, I charged ahead
Daring all roadblocks in sight.
In my strength, I forged ahead
Till all my strength was gone
Deflated like a life vest
Stuck in the middle of the ocean
Gasping for air
Breathing a chore

I'm losing my grip
I'm drowning deep, yet staying afloat.
I open my eyes
and see your strong right arm.
and you... pull me to the shore.

ON MY KNEES: I SEEK

～

On my knees
I pray and praise
With words untold
This world unfolds.

～

On my knees
I sing in awe.
Your voice I crave
Your touch, I feel

On my knees
I seek...
I knock, I ask
My words unfold.
On my knees
I seek
On my knees... I find.

THE COLLAPSE: UNBROKEN DREAMS

~

A rock down in the pit
I fell and hit my head.
the memories far gone
So far I lost my name.
Down in the slums
I felt my father's hand.
I heard my father's voice.
And cowered in pain.
I fell and hit my head...
In flames, I bore no blames
My father's hand, I feel.
the collapse of broken dreams

His love is ever faithful.
His holy presence... ever real
Unbroken dreams... His love restored all.

UNBROKEN VISION

~

All eyes on me
All eyes on you
My life is in you
My trust in you.
Though past in shreds
My faith is ahead.
A future great
Yet so unsure
Chaotic traps
On mountains high
My hope's in you

My faith in you
In bedded thorns
My eyes are on you.

ANOTHER CHANCE TO LIVE

Another chance to live
Another choice to breathe
You've given me
Much more than I can say.
Much more than I can hope
Your love is here to stay.
Though in the midst of thorns
Your grace is what I need.
Another chance to breathe
Another chance to love
Another choice to give
I cherish every day
Another chance with you.

SOLEMN STANCE

Hidden under the sun is none
Without your knowledge
Nothing occurs
My pain you saw ahead.
My gain, you see, you know.
The gain in pain
I question each day
The end is with these soulful pangs...
How far I've come
How far I'll reach...
Depends on you
Enforced by me...
How far I'll reach...
This solemn stance
Your love, your grace
Keeps me each day.

MERCY SPEAKS

Your mercy flows like the ocean.
Have mercy, oh Lord
Have mercy on me
Have mercy on us
On strength delayed
On strength broken
on words unspoken
Have mercy for in weakness
lies your strength.
Have mercy...
In weakness, let your strength reign.
In seasons, lift up your child.
Have mercy because of the thunderstorms.
Have mercy because of this mountain.
The road behind brought turmoil
The road ahead seems vague.
Yet I stand, we will stand...
I trust not in sight.
In the midst of it all
I feel the need to cave
As strength seems frail.
And help so far...
But trust... in you...

In the midst of it all
Strength in need.
Too many roads crossed.
Too many battles won.
few battles lost.
The road behind is blurred by will.
Give up.... a rare word never to be spoken!
This route brings smoke.
As deadly as a serpent bite
Have mercy, and deliver your children!!!
This journey we take
This journey 1 take
In joy, I choose to make
Stay close...
unbreak these wings.
Stand... yes I will still.
Though Lions roar
Press on; I will.

EULOGY

Into a deep abyss
slipping...
Like Alice
I'm in Wonderland.
The shock in my imagination
Reality speaks to my heart.
The pain and disbelief
The pain in my chest
The weakness I feel in me.
Too lethargic to lift them up
To lift her up....any up!
Carry her, you speak.
Carry myself... I cannot
Like times of old
In strength, I prayed.
This time, you know
I seek your face.
I cling with all to you.

To the old rugged cross...
Your arm, I hold
To pull me out.
Though roadblocks come
I'll praise your name.

FIND ME: ANSWERED PRAYERS

Staring out from the deep ocean
A deep sense of loss strikes my heart.
The pain of this cane...
Of lurking through the wilderness too long
I wonder... How the children of Israel felt
I stare out from this wilderness.
An ocean of wilderness...
A desert... lost
We are lost in the wind.
No one can find us
Only you, Father...
Stretch your mighty hand
and pull us out...
From the belly of a whale
As we walk in the storms
Hidden beneath the clouds
a mirror of storms arise
And strangers we see... Find us!
I see you in the storms.
Lost! Find me...
Stabbed a thousand times.
lost sight nursing all wounds
I missed my way trying to find it.

We lost our way, trying to find love, be love.
Lead the way...
Your touch, I need to find me.
Your tour, we need to find us...
Prayers answered find us...
I will sing your praise always.

I WILL TURN TO YOU

When storms arise
When all doors are shut
When open doors are slammed
I will look up to you...

When the world has taken
All it can...
And then... some more!
When left all alone
In the darkest Maze
I will turn to you.

When all I trust is broken
When the steps I strived
So hard to build
The routes I fought too hard
To pave...

Is waved and crushed
I will look unto you...
I will trust in you...

When my foot falters
And my thoughts waver.
And my heart grows...
As cold as ice...
For I see no turn
No one...
I will turn to you...
And sing deep in my heart.

ON THE SUBWAY

Trailing and trailing
Sitting and smiling
The air is rich.
Or not so...
The site is blessed.
The will to live.
The fight to love
To see... to dream.
My dreams are real.
The dreams of past
The thoughts of now
The future's bright
I'll live this life....
I'll live, I'll love
I'll stand through all.
I'll make that mark.
A stamp of faith
My father's grace
Has brought me here.

To share his love!
Sitting and smiling...
Breathing and living.
Thoughts linger of my father.
On the subway.

PART FIVE

THE SOUND OF JOY... BEAUTY FOR ASHES

56 - 70

A THOUSAND SHARES

I died a thousand deaths.
For your love to capture my heart
I cried a thousand tears
To be broken down... Inside out
I'll live a thousand lives
Just to feel your touch over again
I'll go a million miles
To touch your garment
If only... The hem
I'll share a million times
How your love has pulled me through...
Made me stand
Helped me stand...

Your arms, your grace...
A million words I could share...
of your presence in my being.
Your mercy still speaks
Without you...
Into blankness, a way is paved...
So, I will speak a million words
Or more!!!
Walk a million miles.
Your love is immeasurable.
I will share a thousand times!
My father's love is real...

OUT OF THE DUNGEON

In a deep pit, I was
So deep I cannot describe
Words seized
Strength fled
Life interruptions
Life's journey.
In the pit,
in the dungeon
I saw your face
Shining down on me
In the pit, I turned my face
How I got here?
There's no shame...

In the pit, you lift me up
Your love never ceased.
You never cease.
Out of the dungeon...
You lift me up
I hold your hand,
out of the pit...
I'm in your arms.

THE TUNNEL BEACONS

The pain at the edge
The tunnel holds me close
The darkness beacons me.
I see the light
I reach out
It eludes me
My heart is pierced
My mind is dense
The tunnels beacon
The darkness encloses
It gnaws at my heart.
the soul is crushed
Weakened by nature strikes

the valor seeping into the valley
The tunnel beacons...
In you will I trust
Eyes only, on you alone.
The tunnel calls out to me
But into the fathers' light, I will walk in praise.

IN YOUR OCEAN

~

I speak about God's goodness
In likeness to an ocean that runs deep
one I swim in daily
An ocean whose depth I dwell in
I presume... I assume...
I analyze.... I cannot phantom
I can never quantify or understand
The invitation
To swim in your ocean
This is deep
Your ocean sweeps through my veins
Your love for me
Indescribable...

You know my name
You hear my voice
I am your child
And in your ocean, I swim
Day by day.

PRAISE IN THE STORM: TO THE HOLY ONE

∾

In times afar
In times near
In despair and drought
I'll kick fear.
This pruning stance
These nails do sting.
Please hold my hands.
Through stormy waves.

ODE TO THE EAGLE

~

I asked for bread
You gave none
I asked for butter
You had none...
I sourced for scraps.
And found none
I created milk.
I envisioned honey...
I found none...
I see none
In life's end
Or not so ending...
Through life's journey

Don't cry for me
Weep, not my friend
Weep, not my foe
Or rejoice not!
For life's battles made you sour.
The battlefield broke your wings.
It crushed your sight.
With mended wings, go on and fly
Soar with the wind
Forget the pain and tears
Glide and soar... feel the breath of life
So no more tears for you, eagle
No tears for when you crashed...
You asked for scrap... you got none...
I know one who gives all.
And he is beautiful.
Now, spread your wings.
With love
Soar and fly...
On angel wings.

BREATH OF LIFE

~

Breath of life
Fall upon me...
Make me whole again
Make me live again.
Breath of life
Smile upon me... again!
shower rain on us again
Showers of rain...
Healing of pain
Breaking of chains
Walking again.

Breath of life
breathe upon me
Shine upon me
Walk with me
Stand with me...

IN TRIALS, I'LL STAND

In sickness, in health
With gold far from reach
When faced with bricks
I'll stand through all.
Though stand I say
I'm weak and frail
When I can't stand
You lift me up.
When troubles come
Like swarm of bees
When I can't speak
Where feet fail me.
I'll stand and hold on to your grace
I'll stand where bricks
Doth dent my feet
With none in sight
With none to hold
I'll stand and trust
You'll see me through.

ENDEARING PRESENCE

Your love is indescribable.
Your goodness insurmountable
Your grace explicit
Your presence is endearing.
To whom do I share
To whom do I speak
Your goodness towards me
Your mercy holds me firm.
The pits you've lifted me from
The shackles off my feet
You have taken.
You pulled me out of the darkness
An excruciating dark dungeon
Barricaded with chains
In the darkness, with vision blurred
You lifted me out of this and more
Much more than I can describe
Much more than I can phantom.
Your endearing presence I seek each day
You lead, I will follow!

TRIALS...

~

Fear tugs at my heart.
It pierces my mind
The trials of life beats my being
Again... and again
I am weary, I am weak
A knock on my door
Mountains fall as a yoke
choke around the neck
Untangle... I could not
Looking ahead
I see your light once again
This tangle, these ropes
This yoke doth stick
Fear knocks
Trials trail...
All alone...
I am not
All these, I place in your hands.
My eyes are on you; amazing grace
Still, I will praise.
In God I trust!

THE KNOCK: A DOOR MY FATHER SHUT

∼

The irony of a knock
On an enigmatic doorway
The pathway dark and slippery.
When the creeper knocks
All eyes on you...
All words reshaped
The carpenter transforms
In the shape of a coach
The coach tries to be the healer.
The healer stares in confidence
But I see through all
I know the fear; I see all expectations.
Only you know all the stories
Only you know the silence, the story
You see through the heart.
You are my heart!
When the creeper knocked and knocked again
I held your hand,
You shut the door
For I am yours
I will sing to you always.

FOCUSED IN THUNDERSTORMS

The scorn of a maze
a maze once love
the open doors
of loves' great choice.

The scorn of a maze
Where I called home
By whom I called home
From where I saw home.

The mirage of love
In search of my gold
but gold, I have none
and brake lights...
I see none.
Forgiveness is key for mended hearts.

The scorn of a maze
Dejected, not cast off
With eyes fixed on you alone
In whom my trust is in
To you, I sing with faith.

FREE

Free as a bird
My savior doth cover me
Chains have been broken
Shackles taken away.
My savior is here
My savior is near to me
Worries unspoken
He lifts my heavy heart.
He lifts me up
When down and broken.
He sets me free
He keeps on setting me free
Free from dependencies
Free from the yokes that bind
You set me free
My savior doth lift me up.

AN ANGEL YOU SENT

～

You sent me an angel.
You've sent me angels.
Hosts and host...
You sent me a light
To lead me back home
You lead me back home...

～

You sent me an angel.
You heal my soul
My body, my heart.
You gave me strength.
You give strength for each day.

～

A new day, a new dawn
With peace and love
Deep in my heart
Your touch... your light...
Has led me far
Has led me far...

A cocoon you placed
An angel you sent
You held me close.

Your presence, your grace
Your angel, your hand
Your stretched-out arm
Your praise on my lips
An angel you sent
My hand in yours
I stretched out...
And found you...
Your mercy and grace!
I will praise you always.
I will sing your praises all day long.

YOU'VE "BROUGHT" ME "BACK TO LIFE"

My heart was drenched.
My soul wept sore
In the wilderness, I was
Deep, deep... so far gone
In the wilderness
I sang your praises
Lips sore
Heart sore
Heartbroken
Down in the pit
I was lost
Deep in that pit
You found me.
Only you...
You picked me up
Without scorn
You lifted me
And my heart soared
You awakened my soul
Once again
You stretched out
Your ever-loving arms
And there I lay in your presence

I am asked, why do I stand?
My answer: my father is strength
I am asked... why?
I worship you
I call you father
My answer... my story...
your amazing grace
I will praise you forever.
Words cannot express
So I'll sing to you.

PART SIX

RESILLIENCE - IN GOD'S PRESENCE

71-85

WHEN IT RAINS, IT POURS

It rains and pours
raindrops down my cheeks
Down on me
Even when it is over
The rain pours
It rains, it pours
The shadows engulf
Fallen angels beacon
Marauding beasts
gnaw at my heart
I find it hard to breathe
I choke in my own tears.
When it rains, it pours

When would sunshine knock?
Knock on my door once again
I wait for you in silence
A lioness when you speak...
a warrior when you call...
I am still a dove
Heels on my toes
I wait to fly again with you
The sharp pain...
It pierces my soul
Even when it's over
I still feel the storm
It rains, it pours
I shed all tears today
Tears and rain
Drenched in pain
Even though it's over...
The rain is gone
The pain glides away
Now it snows...
And I will stand.

CONTEND

~

Once I knew...
In stillness and calm
Shall be your strength...
This I heard, this I know.
I'm still, I'm calm...
Where does my strength lay?
In calmness?
Storms rage
Locusts came
I did as the masters said
My teachers of old
I waited like "a few good men."
The ones who waited for Captain Godot

Wait and wait, they did
I'm still and calm
But I need to hear from my king
The king of my masters
His voice with no clutters
I know he's near
I'm still, I'm calm
I'm fierce!
I won't wait for Godot... no more.

CENTER

~

Jesus, you are the center
Of my life...
My soul doth long for you
What can I do without you?
Where can I go without you
What can I say
But you are the center...

DANCING ALL THE WAY

~

Dancing all day long
Singing all your praise
Your presence
This joy in my heart I want more of.

~

Your praise in my heart
Your praise, my heart will sing.
In the midst of pain
Pain and sorrow
I Will sing
I Will dance.

Forgetting the pain
Or, in the midst of it all
Come dance with me
The joy in my father's presence
Is indescribable.

KISSING JOY

~

If you could see what I see
If you could dream what I've dreamt
Walk the paths I have walked
Kissed the lips I have kissed
you will feel his joy; that's real
The lips of joy...
Touched the hands of peace
If you can look and see through
The mirrors of my eyes
The mirrors of my soul
My soul longs
My heart weeps

To touch again
To kiss again.
Look into my mirror
And let me breathe...
Free my soul, and let me live.

BREATHING THROUGH THUNDERSTORMS

~

I hold on to your embrace.
Visions evade in cold, cold wars.
A walk in the park
The twist of a knife.
A very long walk through ...wilderness lane.
That walk I never chose to embark on
Who would?
The rear view length is a no-go
The journey ahead... Is a blurry view
The two musketeers tug at my heart
This gentle heart they make stern
The wilderness brings enough storms.
Please let me be so I can breathe.

I'll put my oxygen mask on
I'll have mine on, and so don yours too
so we can both live...
the closet weighs me down too soon
I fight to live well through it all...
Your closets full
But so is mine
Please keep yours shut so I can breathe.

THE VISION

The vision of desolation
When the world is blank
In the bosom of the wilderness
What do we do
What could we do
Where would we stand?
We look to you!

BETTER PLANS

~

Clouds and stormy waves
The mind is as deep as an ocean
Deeper sometimes, I believe
The darkness claws at us
It claws at me
The midgets have no boundaries
I'm out of the deep
Yet they push me further
Shattered, broken
Put together by the potter
The midgets seep through the pores of the soul
They push further into darkness once again
Smiling assassins tug at my heart

To contaminate my soul
They push further into darkness once again
Lest I see your plans!
My focus is on my father.
Your better plans, now I see...
Heart, body, and soul for my father.

HOPE

~

Hope...
She walked out the door.
She left me in chains.
Chains...
I broke them all
Walked out the door
The master...
He walked me through
Now, I stand tall
Tall...
I stood tall
I stand tall...
The chains are gone
Yes, so I thought!
Another race...
Race...
I raced in faith
I raced with hope
Another race!
Please find me hope.

Victory...
My hands held high.
Only my father brings me hope.

THE ROSES TODAY

I do not feel like an eagle today
The scent of the roses does not
Appeal to me
Music once lived in my ears
Like a rainbow path
I walked towards it.
Today, the scent of the roses
Depict an abyss
Tomorrow
I do not know
The Darkness
Engulfing my mind
It will not fold, but I fight
Intentionally
The darkness will not hold.
Today the roses
Appeal not to me
I am an eagle
How do I fly once again
I lost my wings
Need help finding my way.
The scent of the roses
Engulf me

I look ahead
In search of my wings
I will fly again...
I will not fold
I smell the roses
With my hand in yours...

RESCUED FROM THE CLIFF

Look at me...
Look at the depths of who I am
I'm not who I used to be
I'm not who I'm supposed to be.
Touch my life
Pull me from fading into the deep
The smoke did rise against me
The serpents' sting doth
Tarnish my heart
My mind stays firm
My body weak
Look at me, lord
Pull me, save me from the serpent bite
Crush the scorpions' sting
The scorpions' sting
The challenges... do increase
The snake never left.
He lurked In the shadows
Like a thief in the night.
I am at the edge of the cliff!
You rescued me and crushed the serpent's being.

JOY WITHIN: HAPPY BUTTERFLY

~

A walk through the valley
The shadows arise
Tables set before me
The veils covered my eyes.
Sweep over my soul once again
Fill me with joy within
That joy down in my heart
I long for once again
Walking through this valley
I thought...
Joy was gone, replaced with
Anger and cold, cold snares
The joy you give...
Is lasting, everlasting
I hold onto you once again
And feel your warm embrace
I praise, I raise
Your name on high
I share...
Your love, your truth

You are good all the time.
I unlock shut doors
The joy within springs forth
Please bring to life again... this happy butterfly!

LIKE A SPRINKLER

Like a sprinkler
Teardrops
Trips down memory lane
The boulevard of broken dreams
The promise to unbreak
To stand to soar...
Nothing is promised
But God is still good
I recollect
Nothing Is Permanent
Like a sprinkler
The tears roll down once again
I search for the street
I heard her name is Hope
On this lonely road, I walk
I never chose...
Like a sprinkler
Teardrops on thorns or roses
My bed I will pick up...
And walk.
Like a sprinkler!

MY FATHERS' FEET

~

Open up my heart, lord
So I may hear your voice
Open up my ears, lord
So I may listen to your words

~

I long for your embrace.
How good it feels in your embrace
I lay down at your feet
And drift away
My mind is blank
My soul in draft
I break the chains and walk away...

THE TOUCH FROM THE HOLY ONE

The sea calls out
Too many... But none to answer
This weary heart
This battered bones
The sea calls out again
Inviting its prey
Its beauty is beyond my thoughts
My thoughts are mush and squash
A snap of faith
Brings me to life
But... the sea calls out to me
It pulls me close
I'm by the shore
The edge?
There's sand beneath my feet
The sea calls out, so I walk in...
the presence of my father sweeps through the sea
sweeps over my being
His voice, his touch
Relieves me from the sea.
Just lift your heart and let him in.

PART SEVEN

ABUNDANCE OF RAIN WITH PRAISE

86 - 100

GRACE UNBROKEN

A knot in my heart
The thirst in my soul
What's real
What's not
Yet grace abounds
A smile on the lips
A smile from the heart?
The melting heart
Unmelt my heart
What's real, what's not
Who's real, Who's not
Points of no return

Words unspoken
Pain unbroken?
Grace untainted, unbroken
Through grief and pain
Your presence is real.

MY FATHERS' PRESENCE

Gold and silver to give, I have not
Riches like never seen on earth
I have none to give
The love of my father
Yes, I can share
So now I give that which I have...
The greatest gift
My father's love
I introduce you to my king.
He makes me... me...
He'll make you... you.
Just lift your heart and let him in.

EVERYTHING

~

Jesus, you are everything.
In the darkness
You shine through and bring me to your light
All my sacrifices and work mean nothing
Without your presence
Everything means nothing...
Without your presence.
Our father... let your presence reign...
in all the earth... let it rain
with drops of hope and oceans of love.

THE MOUNTAIN WHISTLES

~

The heavens and the earth
Shake for my sake
The mountains whistle
The seas roar
God is for me
He stands with me
The angels sing for my sake
The wars try to engulf
But the angels fight for me
Though I feel weak
From the attacking marauders
Beasts of the Night

From the battlefields
The fierce battles...
I will stand
I will sing
God is for me.

HERE WE GO AGAIN

~

Here we go again.
Now, I say we
Because I'm not alone
The fear is gone
The peace is here to stay
The battle, not done
The thought of a finished battle
I hoped I had finished the fight
The belief, the hope
I put down my armors.
Here we go again!

My armors... I pick up once again...
And stand? Yes I will
We walk through time and space.

ACKNOWLEDGE

～

With a smile, a hug
Acknowledge
The good deeds done
With a word
Of love, not hate
Acknowledge
The past fog has gone
With a gift
Save a life
With a smile
Melt a heart
Acknowledge the good
Acknowledge

And not put down.
With a smile
Lend a hand
If one Is down
Lift him up.

NEW SONG

~

Seasons come and go
Aberrations of grandeur
Illusions, creations
A Season in the Battlefield
A season in the midst of a battle
The purpose, the reason
We analyze day by day
Seasons come and go
My father is here to stay
New seasons
New Songs

The reason?
Unknown...
Yet... I decree, I declare, and I dance...
My father's presence is here!

SPRING

~

My love has come back to me
It's springtime
The roses bloom
My heart is filled with joy!
The pain and sorrow melt away
Yet tears strip down my cheeks.
It's springtime!
And once again, you wipe away my tears
My heart is entwined in yours
Tears of relief and joy fill my soul
The spring was near...
The spring is here...

So is your love and embrace!
My hand in yours once again
It's spring in my heart once again.

I AM THE REDEEMED OF THE LORD

I wake up to you today...
To your loving kindness each day
Mountains may rise
Oceans may roar
Seasons come and go
Oceans may roar
Lions and tigers...
May trail on a rail
I wake up to you
To see your goodness
Through waves...
In and out of seasons
Your touch calms my being
Your love engulfs like a stream
Like an ocean
Immeasurable, uncontained.
I wake up to your goodness!
You are my deliverer, amazing God!
I am the redeemed of the lord
And I say so...

FROM THE LAND OF NOT

~

The land of not and blankness
Trading in cycles
The garden and the cross
My mind swirling and twirling
I surrender; I escape the land of Not.

~

The land of not and blankness
My breathing evades the darkness
The Joy of the Father
The joy in the Father brings me from
Blankness...

~

Surreal or not, all is vanity.
Each realm connotes the kingdom's reign.
Each life, each death
The potter knows
In life, with joy, remove each veil.

MY HEART IS TROUBLED

My heart is troubled
I long for peace
Peppermint in the air
Breathing is the life
Fighting with a cause
Fighting for a cause?
My heart is troubled
The spring is here
Though summer is near
Tensions still arise...
My heart is troubled
Please heal our souls
In God we trust.

FLIGHT PLAN UNTAMED

When all routes turn bleak
When all turns grey
And the world is greasy
Your efforts uneasy
In crisis and vices
The hurt is revealed
The warm embraces grow cold
Piercing the heart and soul
All veils unfold
Of wars to fold
All the tears are still
Lest we drift into blankness.
As all is said, what is done?
The veil is still on
The warm embrace has gone cold.
I stood, I fought
Flight plan untamed
A blade so sharp.
I fell, I stood.
There is a purpose for all...
I crawled back to my father's arms.

HOSANNA

Have mercy, oh lord
The human mind is fleeting
Like waves on mittens
Our hearts stutter and waver.

Have mercy, oh lord,
With these same lips
We hailed
"Hosanna, save us."
With our lips, our hands
Our hearts and deeds
We crucified
Our fleeting hearts
Our heedless minds
We forget once you save.

Have mercy, oh lord!
The errors of our ways

The errors of a nation
The errors of people
The errors of a person?
Opened doors to a land of ...dreary
Lands and nations
People and persons
Let the wave pass over us
Cleanse the errors
Let joy once again reign
We will not forget
I will not forget

Have Mercy, Oh Lord
Save us once again
And this time, we will write your laws and love
In our hearts
In our souls
We will speak and embrace the truth
so it may set us free

Have Mercy, Oh Lord
We will remember your goodness
And how you saved us from man's errors

Let the resurrection power arise once again
And cleanse all lands
Let your power reign
Hosanna let this wave pass
We will praise you always.

OUR REDEEMER

~

Lilies and Roses
Foxes and bridges
My soul, they tried to take
My mind was driven into blankness
Plagues and waves
Droughts and lanes
A long road I see ahead
My mind still I fight to keep
My soul, the lords to hold
Literary waves
Seep through my being
Medium... my eyes
My ears
Then my thoughts
My soul, they try to steal
My mind is not blankness
The Lord keeps
The gate crashers never sleep
Please wake up
Wake me up
Unscale my eyes
Unveil my mind

Hand-made or man-made
We hold on to you
We call out your name to save.
Through sorrow and pain
Our strength... your joy!

A TIME FOR PRAISE

For a time like this
Live in praise
Live for praise
Live to praise.

For a time like this
Look up to Christ
Rest in the father's arms
You can lay all day long.

For a time like this
A season, reason unknown
A spiral, a tunnel
The end or a new beginning?

For a time like this
Lean on his love
Tunnel or funnel.

SHARE YOUR SONG

Thank you for letting these words come alive in your hearts in every way; I believe they will inspire you to breathe, fight, stand, and not give up...... in all seasons. Speak words of love, joy, and peace. Sing and share your songs with the father.

ABOUT THE AUTHOR

~

Lola Ahmed is a lifelong poet, visionary, and Child of God. She is also an entrepreneur and Subject Matter Expert in different sectors, with a passion for positively impacting this generation and future generations.

"Songs for My Father" is a poetry collection of hope to God that identifies the presence of pain and joy in many seasons in this journey called life, and the ability to speak to the Father in all seasons. Its purpose is to share and empower, using poetry to illustrate the ability to walk, speak, praise, and have genuine conversations with God in and through all seasons. This poetry sequence identifies the reality of pain in some seasons, hope and faith that keep us firm, and love and resilience that gives us the courage to not give up in any season for any reason.

www.ingramcontent.com/pod-product-compliance
Lightning Source LLC
Chambersburg PA
CBHW070927250626
47159CB00009B/3150